Who Is
Aaron Judge?

Who Is
Aaron Judge?

by James Buckley Jr.

illustrated by Andrew Thomson

Penguin Workshop

This one's for Bill,
the world's biggest Yankees fan—JB

For Rhia, Cerys, and Baby Girl to be—AT

PENGUIN WORKSHOP
An imprint of Penguin Random House LLC, New York

First published in the United States of America by Penguin Workshop,
an imprint of Penguin Random House LLC, New York, 2024

Visit us online at penguinrandomhouse.com.

Library of Congress Cataloging-in-Publication Data is available.

Printed in the United States of America

ISBN 9780593750131 (paperback)   10 9 8 7 6 5 4 3 2 1 WOR
ISBN 9780593750148 (library binding)   10 9 8 7 6 5 4 3 2 1 WOR

Contents

Who Is Aaron Judge?

Fans of the New York Yankees *really* don't like the Boston Red Sox. The two teams have been fierce rivals for more than a century. A Yankees fan's two favorite teams are the Yankees . . . and whoever is playing against the Red Sox. If that is true, then why, late in the 2022 season, were fans at Yankee Stadium actually *cheering* for the Red Sox to score? This unusual situation came up because Yankees slugger Aaron Judge would get another chance to hit only if Boston tied the game . . . and he'd get another chance at tying an all-time home run record. Yankees fans had been cheering for Aaron all season, and they hoped he would tie and break the record in his home stadium. Aaron appreciated their support.

"Seeing Yankee Stadium on their feet for every single at-bat [was amazing]," Aaron said. "They were booing pitchers for throwing balls [out of the strike zone], which I've never seen before."

Game after game in a short series of games, however, Red Sox pitchers avoided throwing Aaron good pitches. The fans booed that, too! In one game, the fans groaned in frustration even when Aaron hit a double—usually something worth cheering. It wasn't a homer, so it wasn't what they wanted. In another game, fans in Yankees shirts shouted, "Let's go, Red Sox!" as Boston tried to tie the score to force extra innings. (It didn't work.) Finally, in the last game of that Red Sox series, the crowd went home sad and wet when Aaron didn't hit a homer and the game ended due to rain after only six innings, three short of a normal game.

That meant Yankees fans—and baseball lovers everywhere—had to keep waiting. Then, on September 28, he hit his 61st homer; that tied the American League (AL) and Yankees record set by Roger Maris in 1961. Roger's son was in the stands in Toronto to watch that big moment. Aaron needed one more home run to break the record. The season was almost over. Would there be enough games left for him to break the record? Yankees fans held their breath as Aaron went into a home run slump! Game after game, he didn't hit one out.

In the Yankees' second-to-last game, they were in Texas to play the Rangers. Aaron led off the game against right-hander Jesus Tinoco. On the third pitch, Aaron blasted a long drive (a ball hit a great distance) to left field. The ball flew on and on . . . and out! It was a home run, number 62 of the season! Aaron had done it! He was the new AL home run champ!

Here's the story about the amazing path from small-town hero to big-league superstar, the story of the rise of Aaron Judge.

CHAPTER 1
Finding a Family

On April 26, 1992, Aaron James Judge was born in Linden, California. Linden is a small farming community about ninety miles east of San Francisco. The town is famous for its cherry trees.

When he was just two days old, Aaron was adopted by Wayne and Patty Judge. The Judge family already had a son, John, who had been adopted seven years earlier.

Aaron's parents were teachers, and early on they made him focus on education. Aaron had other ideas. "I wanted to go outside and play with my friends or play some video games, but they were tough on me," he remembered later. "They'd say, 'Hey, you've got homework to do.

If you have time left over before dinner, you can go play.'"

Aaron loved to play. There was not a sport he was not good at. He grew quickly and was soon among the biggest kids in his neighborhood.

But as he grew, he also noticed that he did not look like his parents. Aaron was biracial, but his parents were white. When Aaron was about ten, he asked them about it. Wayne and Patty told Aaron that both he and John had been adopted. "I was fine with it," he said many years later. "It really didn't bother me because [they're] the only parents I've known." Aaron said that after they had that talk, he went right out to play!

Later, Aaron said he felt being adopted made him appreciate his parents even more. "I have one set of parents, the ones that raised me. Some kids grow in their mom's stomach; I grew in my mom's heart."

Meanwhile, Aaron learned a lot about sports from his father. Along with being a teacher, Wayne was the Linden High School basketball coach. Aaron often went to practices to help out as a ball boy. Being around older players helped shape Aaron's ideas about the game. He saw the hard work that Wayne's teams put in. He also had fun when they let him take some

shots. In middle school, Aaron was six feet tall,
bigger than some of the high-school players!

By the time he reached high school himself,
Aaron was more than six feet, three inches tall
and still growing. He joined the Linden High
School Lions teams for basketball, baseball, and
football, and became a star for all three sports.
Though Wayne was no longer the basketball

coach, Aaron excelled, using his height to set scoring records. As a senior, he averaged 18.2 points per game and was named to an all-state team. In football, Aaron's size made him a great receiver. He was able to leap above opponents or use his strength to break tackles. He set a school record with 17 touchdowns in his final season.

Aaron enjoyed baseball more than the other sports. He mostly played first base, but he also pitched for the Lions. As a hitter, his batting average topped .500, which means he got a hit at least every other official at bat. He began crushing long home runs, some that his coaches said went five hundred feet or more!

Opposing teams often just walked Aaron rather than give him a chance to hit another homer. Aaron's focus on working hard continued, even as he excelled. His high-school coaches remember that after almost every game, win or lose, Aaron asked to take extra batting practice to work on his swing.

While he was at Linden High, Aaron also began a lifetime habit of helping out. He and his basketball teammates would regularly pick up trash around the community.

With so much athletic talent, Aaron was recruited by colleges in all three sports, especially for football. Powerhouse schools like the University of Notre Dame and UCLA offered him scholarships. "I thought about going the football route," Aaron said later. "But I saw myself having fun playing baseball for the rest of my life."

California State University, Fresno—known

as Fresno State—was only about a two-hour drive from Linden. Wayne and Patty Judge had graduated from that college. Aaron went to a baseball camp there, and coach Mike Batesole was impressed. "He took like three swings. I said, 'Forget the rest of camp, are your mom and dad here?' We offered him a scholarship right then and there."

In the fall of 2010, Aaron became a Fresno State Bulldog.

CHAPTER 2
The Road to Yankee Stadium

The move up to college baseball helped Aaron improve his skills even more. One of his high-school coaches, Leif Nilsen, said that playing at Fresno State really helped Aaron get the right training to aim at the major leagues. Aaron hit .358 in his first season and was named a Freshman All-American. He helped the Bulldogs win a second straight conference championship in 2012. That July, Aaron won the College Home Run Derby. In front of fans from around the country, he smashed 16 homers in three rounds. Aaron also continued to learn to be a good teammate. At Fresno State, players had to pay a dollar every time they boasted about doing something or used "I" or "my" too often in interviews. That taught Aaron to put the team first.

In the summer of 2012, Aaron played for the Brewster Whitecaps in the Cape Cod Baseball League in Massachusetts. Some of the best college players in the country spend the summer in that league, improving their skills. They play with wood bats, which are not used in college but are used in professional baseball. Working with wood bats is an adjustment players need to make to reach the majors. Aaron used his time to get better at hitting homers. During an event at Boston's Fenway Park, home of the Red Sox, Aaron amazed scouts from major-league teams with a power display, launching very long home runs. He had one more college season to play, but it was clear to experts that his future was as a professional player.

Aaron learned a lot in Cape Cod, and in 2013, his third year at Fresno State, he smashed 12 homers in 56 games. That was three times as many as he had hit in any previous college season. In the summer of 2013, the Yankees made him their first-round choice in the MLB Amateur Draft, an event at which teams select high-school and college players. Aaron got a signing bonus of $1.8 million, thrilling his parents and all of his fans back in Linden. Unfortunately, while training before joining the Yankees' minor-league team, Aaron tore a muscle in his leg. He had to miss nearly a year while he recovered.

In 2014, he reported to Yankees' camp in Florida, ready to show what he could do. He was assigned uniform number 99; most rookies are given very high numbers. When they make the major leagues, they often change to a lower number. Aaron, however, grew to love his unique digits and still wears 99 today.

No matter how high a player is drafted, nearly all of them spend time in the minor leagues, adjusting to life as a pro. Aaron played for the

Tampa Yankees and the Charleston RiverDogs at the Single-A level in 2014. In 2015, he moved up to the Double-A level with the Trenton Thunder, and then to the Triple-A with the Scranton/Wilkes-Barre RailRiders.

Aaron had lots of homers and long hits while in the minor leagues, but he also had a lot of strikeouts—he hit 56 homers, but he struck out 373 times.

The Yankees still felt he would be a big leaguer. In mid-August 2016, Aaron had just finished a game for the RailRiders in Rochester, New York, when he got the call that he was wanted at Yankee Stadium the next day.

Aaron and his parents, who had been visiting him, drove through the night to reach the big city. Wayne and Patty were in the stands on August 13, 2016, when Aaron, in his first major-league at bat with the Yankees, hit a home run!

Aaron's first major-league home run was a thrilling moment, but in other big-league games the rest of that 2016 season, there were few others like it. Aaron hit only three more homers that season . . . and struck out a total of

42 times. His batting average was only .179. Aaron had great potential, but that short visit to the big leagues with the Yankees showed him that he had a lot to learn, too.

CHAPTER 3
All Rise!

On his cell phone, Aaron keeps a picture of the number .179 to look at for motivation. He always wants to remember his struggles during his first taste of the major leagues. He doesn't want to repeat them.

When Aaron started in right field for the Yankees at the beginning of the 2017 season, baseball had never seen anyone like him. He became a rare non-pitcher who was more than six and a half feet tall.

Aaron showed that he had learned his lessons. He started blasting homers—he had 15 in his first 40 games. But it was not all long balls. Aaron was becoming a better overall hitter. For most of the season, his batting average was above .300. He still struck out a lot, but when he hit the ball . . . it went a long way.

Yankees fans were thrilled by their young slugger. Teammate Todd Frazier quickly gave Aaron a nickname that fans came to love. "All rise!" is the call for people to stand when a judge enters a courtroom, and when Aaron hit a homer, that's what all the Yankees fans did, too—rise up out of their seats. To take advantage of Aaron's popularity—and his last name— the ball club set up a special set of seats in right field, where many of his homers were landing. The Judge's Chambers, as the area was called, had fake wood walls, and fans sitting there were given black judges' robes and foam gavels. (*Chambers* is the word for a judge's office.)

While fans were settling into the Chambers, Aaron was trying to find a place in New York City.

At first, he roomed with fellow outfielder Brett Gardner, a Yankees veteran. Gardner's kids once complained when Aaron ate some of their Easter candy! Aaron later moved into a hotel room for

most of the season. When asked why he didn't
rent an apartment, he said, "Maybe next year, if
everything goes well."

Everything went very well for Aaron. The home

runs kept flying, as the baseball world discovered this powerful, humble slugger. At a game against Baltimore, fans marveled when Aaron hit a 496-foot homer, his longest ever. A day earlier, he had hit a ball that went 121.1 miles per hour off his bat, the highest speed ever recorded to that point.

Still, even Yankees fans didn't always recognize their young hero. For a TV show, Aaron put on glasses and interviewed fans in New York City, showing them a photo of himself. Many of the fans had great things to say about Aaron, but they didn't realize they were right beside him!

By July 7, he had hit 30 homers. That broke the Yankees rookie record, set in 1936 by Hall of Famer Joe DiMaggio. Meanwhile, Aaron created a pregame ritual that he continues today. Before each game, he tosses forty sunflower seeds onto the field, one for each of the players on his team's extended roster. Then he says a short prayer and gets to work.

That July, Aaron got more votes from fans for the All-Star Game than any other American League player! Aaron was also invited to take part in the Home Run Derby. The annual contest is held the day before the All-Star Game. A select group of sluggers aims for the fences on pitches served up by handpicked partners. The pitches are much easier to hit than in a regular game, but it still takes timing, talent, and power to hit so many home runs. Watched by the other sluggers in the derby, Aaron put on a show. He smacked 23 homers to win the first round. Four of his homers in the derby went more than five hundred feet! He made it to the final round where he hit another 11 massive long balls to defeat Miguel Sanó of the Minnesota Twins. Aaron became the second rookie ever to win.

For his part, Aaron remained his humble self, praising his derby pitcher, coach Danilo Valiente, and remembering others. "I have had wonderful people help me out through the years. And I can't thank them enough for where I'm at right now."

Aaron kept slugging as the season went on and aimed toward beating the single-season record for rookies, 49 homers set by Mark McGwire of the Oakland A's in 1987. But Aaron ended July with just 34 homers and hit only three in August. In early September, however, he got his home run swing back.

On September 25, Aaron hit two homers against the Kansas City Royals at Yankee Stadium.

Home Run Derby

Baseball fans love watching home runs. Sluggers like Aaron Judge love hitting them. Put those two things together and you get the annual Home Run Derby. This popular contest is held on the Monday before the MLB All-Star Game, usually in July. Four players from each league face off in a playoff format. Players choose their pitchers, selecting people who would provide easy balls to hit. Each player is given a short time period to hit as many long balls as possible. The winners of each round advance toward a final showdown.

The first Home Run Derby was held in 1985. Over the years, many future Hall of Famers have won the derby, including Cal Ripken Jr., Frank Thomas, and Ken Griffey Jr., who won it three times. Some derbies also raised money for charities.

Recent winners include Pete "Polar Bear"

Alonso of the New York Mets, who won in 2019 and 2021. Also in 2021, Shohei Ohtani of the Los Angeles Angels was the first player from Japan to take part. In 2022, Juan Soto, then of the Washington Nationals, became the second-youngest winner.

That gave him 50 on the season, setting a new all-time rookie record. As fans chanted his name, humble Aaron was forced out of the dugout by his joyous teammates to take the first curtain call of his career.

Aaron ended the 2017 season with 52 homers to lead the American League. His 33 homers hit in Yankees home games broke a record set by the great Babe Ruth. That year, Aaron was the unanimous winner of the Jackie Robinson AL Rookie of the Year Award. He also won his first Silver Slugger as the best AL hitter at his position.

Showing that even a great player has room to improve, Aaron also set a new MLB rookie record with 208 strikeouts.

CHAPTER 4
Home Run Hero

In 2018, Aaron's second full season with the Yankees, he once again made the American League All-Star team. However, in July, he broke a bone in his wrist when it was hit by a pitch. Aaron had to miss almost two months of the season. He ended the year with just 27 home runs.

During the season, though, he and his parents created the All Rise Foundation as a way to give back. All Rise raises money to send kids in Linden to baseball and leadership camps. As his career continued, Aaron's foundation also helped other kids in Fresno, New York City, and other places. Patty Judge is still one of the foundation's leaders.

Back on the field, Aaron had another bumpy

Aaron leads a baseball camp

season in 2019. He hit 27 homers again and won an award for defense, but an injury to a muscle in his side limited him to only 102 of the Yankees' 162 games.

Just before the 2020 season, the COVID-19 pandemic shut down all sports, including Major League Baseball. The Yankees' season didn't start until July 23 and lasted only 60 games. Aaron got off to a hot start, hitting seven homers in the team's first ten games. Then another injury hurt a muscle in his calf. He played only 28 of the team's games in that shortened season.

Finally, in 2021, Aaron played a full, injury-free season for the first time since 2017. He cracked 39 homers, made the All-Star team, and won his second Silver Slugger Award.

In the off-season, Aaron and the Yankees tried to agree on a new contract. The team really wanted their star slugger to stay for a long time. They offered him $213 million for seven seasons. Aaron, however, thought he might be able to make more on a longer contract. He agreed to a one-year deal for 2022. If he had a great season, then he would probably be offered much more money by the Yankees or some other team. He was taking a risk. If he had a bad 2022, he might never be offered that much again!

Before the 2022 season began, however, the Judge family celebrated a big event. In December 2021, Aaron married Samantha Bracksieck in Hawaii. Aaron had begun dating Samantha when he was in high school in Linden.

As the 2022 season began, Aaron showed that he had made the right choice by believing in himself. But it took a while to get started; he didn't hit his first homer until the team's sixth game. Then the homers came in bunches. One of his homers came on April 26, his thirtieth birthday. On May 3 in Toronto, a home run ball hit by Aaron was caught by a Blue Jays fan who then gifted the ball to a young boy in a Yankees shirt. Video of the moment went viral, and Aaron met the boy and the generous fan the next day. The boy was wearing a 99 shirt. "It still gives me goose bumps seeing little kids wearing my number," Aaron said.

On June 3, he became the first player to reach 20 homers in 2022, and he reached 33 homers by the time of the All-Star break on July 17.

On July 28, Aaron hit his third walk-off home run of the season, hitting a blast in the team's last turn at bat to give the Yankees a win over the Kansas City Royals.

As the homer count rose, fans and baseball experts started wondering if Aaron could break the MLB single-season record of 73, set by Barry Bonds of the San Francisco Giants in 2001. Aaron also took aim at the AL record of 61 home runs, set in 1961 by Roger Maris of the Yankees in a famous home-run battle with teammate Mickey Mantle.

Aaron reached 50 homers for the second time in his career on August 29, kicking off a remarkable stretch of games. In the Yankees' next 18 games, Aaron hit 10 homers! Two came in one game against the rival Boston Red Sox, home runs 56 and 57.

At Yankee Stadium on September 20, Aaron tied the great Babe Ruth's 1927 mark of 60 homers. But then Aaron went seven games without a homer.

His teammates continued to crowd the top of the dugout steps to get a good view of every at bat by Aaron. They poured onto the field to celebrate when he finally got number 61 in Toronto on September 28, tying Maris. "It was just a really good moment of togetherness," said pitcher Gerrit Cole. "We're all so proud of him and know how hard he works."

1961: Maris vs. Mantle

In 2022, Aaron Judge was aiming for the American League single-season home run record of 61. That mark had been set in 1961 by another Yankee slugger, Roger Maris. That season, Maris and teammate Mickey Mantle put on one of the great home run battles in baseball history. Both were aiming at 60 homers, the record at that time. It was set by another legendary Yankee, Babe Ruth, back in 1927.

Maris and Mantle started crushing homers in bunches as the 1961 season began. By the end of June, both hitters were ahead of Ruth's pace. Fans and writers followed each at bat eagerly. Which slugger would reach the famous record? Some saw the two as bitter rivals, but the "M&M Boys" were actually roommates in a New York City apartment and supported each other.

The race was tight until Mantle was injured in September. He wound up with 53 homers. Maris went on to hit his 61st home run on the final day of the season, an AL record that would last until 2022.

Roger Maris and Mickey Mantle

Aaron needed just one more to break the AL record, but he went five more games without hitting a home run, including three games at Yankee Stadium. Time was running out on the season and Aaron's home run chase.

Finally, in the Yankees' second-to-last game, Aaron did it. At Globe Life Field, home of the Texas Rangers, in Arlington, Texas, he hit a homer off pitcher Jesus Tinoco of the Rangers. It was the 62nd long ball of the season for Aaron, setting a new American League and Yankees team record. Fans in Texas stood and cheered, knowing they had seen history even if it was against their team. Aaron was surrounded by his teammates again, all of them eager to share in the fun and congratulate him. After the game, Aaron said, "It's a big relief. I think everybody can finally sit down in their seats and watch the ball game."

Aaron ended the 2022 regular season leading

the major leagues with 62 homers, 131 RBI (runs batted in: a stat that measures when you get a hit that brings a teammate in to score), and 133 runs scored. His slugging average (a measure of hitting power) was also tops at .686. He won his third Silver Slugger, and in November, was named the AL Most Valuable Player.

As much as Aaron enjoyed breaking the record and earning awards, he did not enjoy the 2022 postseason games as much. The Yankees made the playoffs, but Aaron hit only .139 in two series and struck out 15 times. He even made the last out in the final loss to the Houston Astros in the AL Championship Series.

Not long after the season, Aaron's gamble on his contract paid off. In December 2022, he signed a new contract with the Yankees for $360 million over nine years, one of the biggest deals in baseball history! Yankees fans were thrilled!

That also means that as Aaron keeps crushing home runs to help his team, his All Rise Foundation will keep helping, too. He says that he hopes to help kids "reach unlimited possibilities." With the way he hits homers, Aaron has no limits on possibilities on the baseball field, either!

Baseball's Fiercest Rivalry

Boston Red Sox fans don't like the New York Yankees because, for almost a century, the Yankees regularly crushed the Red Sox. Yankees fans don't like the Red Sox, either, but in the 2000s, the Red Sox have come out on top. No matter who is winning, the two teams make up baseball's biggest rivalry.

The rivalry really began in 1920 when the Red Sox traded the great hitter Babe "the Bambino" Ruth to the Yankees. Ruth went on to help the Yankees win four World Series championships. The team added more titles in every decade of the 1900s except the 1980s, until they had won 26 through 2000. Meanwhile, under what was called the "Curse of the Bambino," the Red Sox won zero. To make things worse, the Yankees beat the Red Sox in several playoff series.

Babe Ruth

Then in 2004, Boston broke through. They beat
New York in an AL playoff and then won their first
World Series championship in 86 seasons (they had
last won in 1918 . . . when Ruth was on their team!).
The Red Sox won the Series again in 2007, 2013, and
2018, while the Yankees won only in 2009. The Sox
have a long way to go to catch the Yankees, but
they'll keep fighting!

Timeline of Aaron Judge's Life

1992 — Born on April 26 in Linden, California

2010 — Plays as a star athlete on three high-school sports teams (football, baseball, and basketball)

2011 — Named Freshman All-American at Fresno State

2013 — Drafted in the first round of the MLB Amateur Draft by the New York Yankees

2014 — After missing a year due to injury, begins playing in the minor leagues

2016 — Makes his major-league debut with the Yankees and hits a home run in his first at bat

2017 — In July, voted by fans as a starter in the All-Star Game and wins Home Run Derby

— Sets MLB rookie record with 52 homers

— Wins Jackie Robinson AL Rookie of the Year Award

2021 — Makes All-Star Game for the third time

— In December, marries Samantha Bracksieck

2022 — Sets new AL and Yankees team record with 62 homers

— In November, named AL Most Valuable Player

— In December, signs new nine-year contract with the Yankees

Timeline of the World

1991 — The first post is made to the World Wide Web, in Switzerland

1994 — The Channel Tunnel opens, linking France and Great Britain

2001 — Barry Bonds of the San Francisco Giants sets a major-league record with 73 homers

2004 — A tsunami hits Indonesia and other countries, killing about 230,000 people and causing billions of dollars in damage

2007 — Apple releases the first iPhone

2008 — Barack Obama elected first Black president of the United States

2014 — *Philae*, a European space probe, becomes the first spacecraft to land on a comet

2015 — Nearly two hundred countries sign the Paris Climate Agreement to deal with climate change

2016 — Great Britain votes to leave the European Union, a process known as Brexit

2020 — COVID-19 pandemic strikes the world, killing millions and creating widespread economic problems

2022 — Russia invades Ukraine

Bibliography

*Books for young readers

"Aaron Judge." *Britannica Kids Online*. https://kids.britannica.
com/students/article/Aaron-Judge/635438.

*Bates, Greg. *Aaron Judge: Baseball Star*. Lake Elmo, MN:
Focus Readers, 2019.

*Buckley, James Jr. *Show Me History: Babe Ruth: Baseball's All-
Time Best!* San Diego: Portable Press, 2020.

*Fishman, Jon M. *Aaron Judge*. Sports All-Stars. Minneapolis:
Lerner, 2019.

Goldman, Dylan. "Rookie Aaron Judge Dominates MLB Home Run
Derby." *Sports Illustrated Kids*. July 11, 2017. https://www.
sikids.com/kid-reporter/rookie-aaron-judge-dominates-
mlb-home-run-derby.

Schoenfeld, David. "The Road to 62: How Aaron Judge Made Home
Run History in 2022." *ESPN.com*. October 4, 2022. https://
www.espn.com/mlb/story/_/id/34534861/new-york-yankees-
aaron-judge-home-run-record.

Website

Aaron Judge's Official Major League Baseball statistics page:
https://www.mlb.com/player/aaron-judge-592450